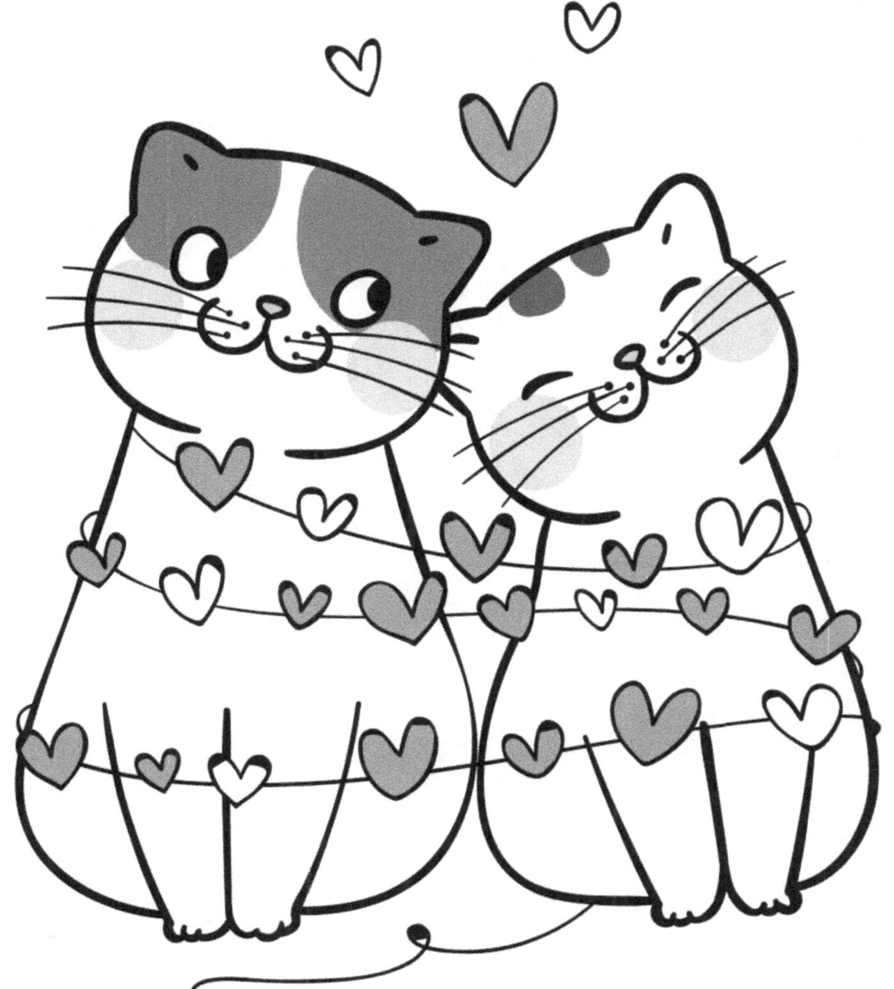

THIS BOOK BELONG TO ....

....

....

....

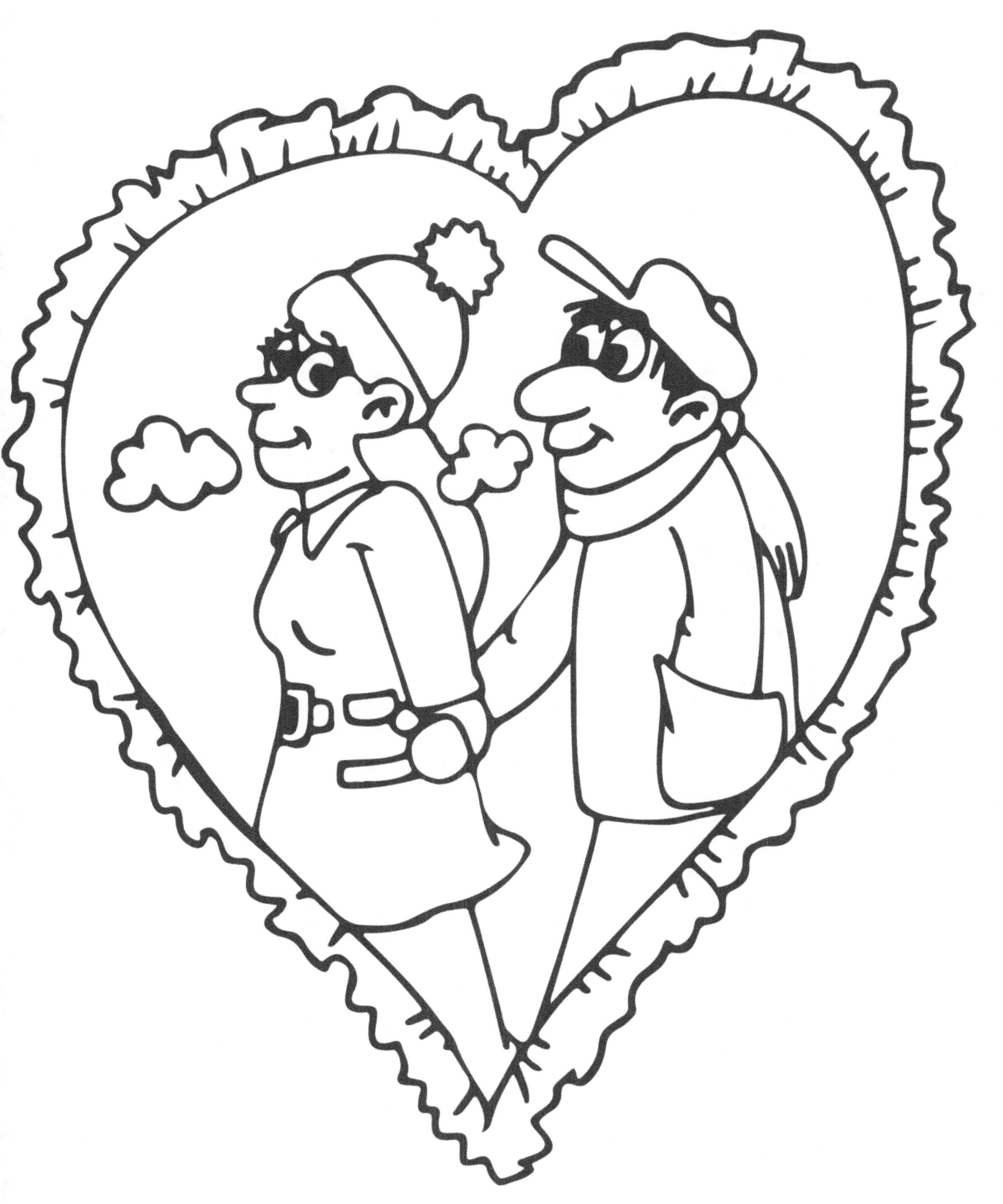

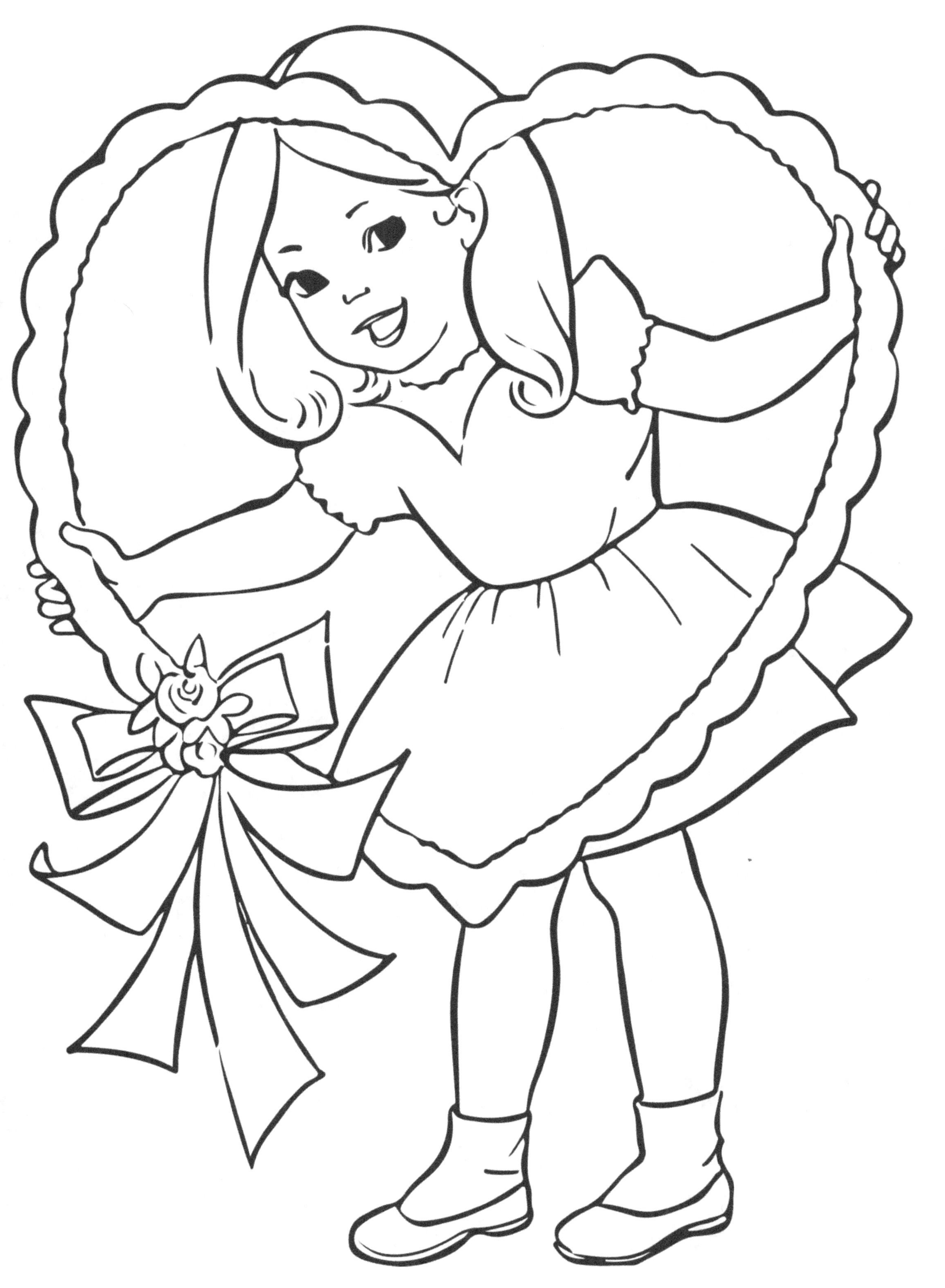

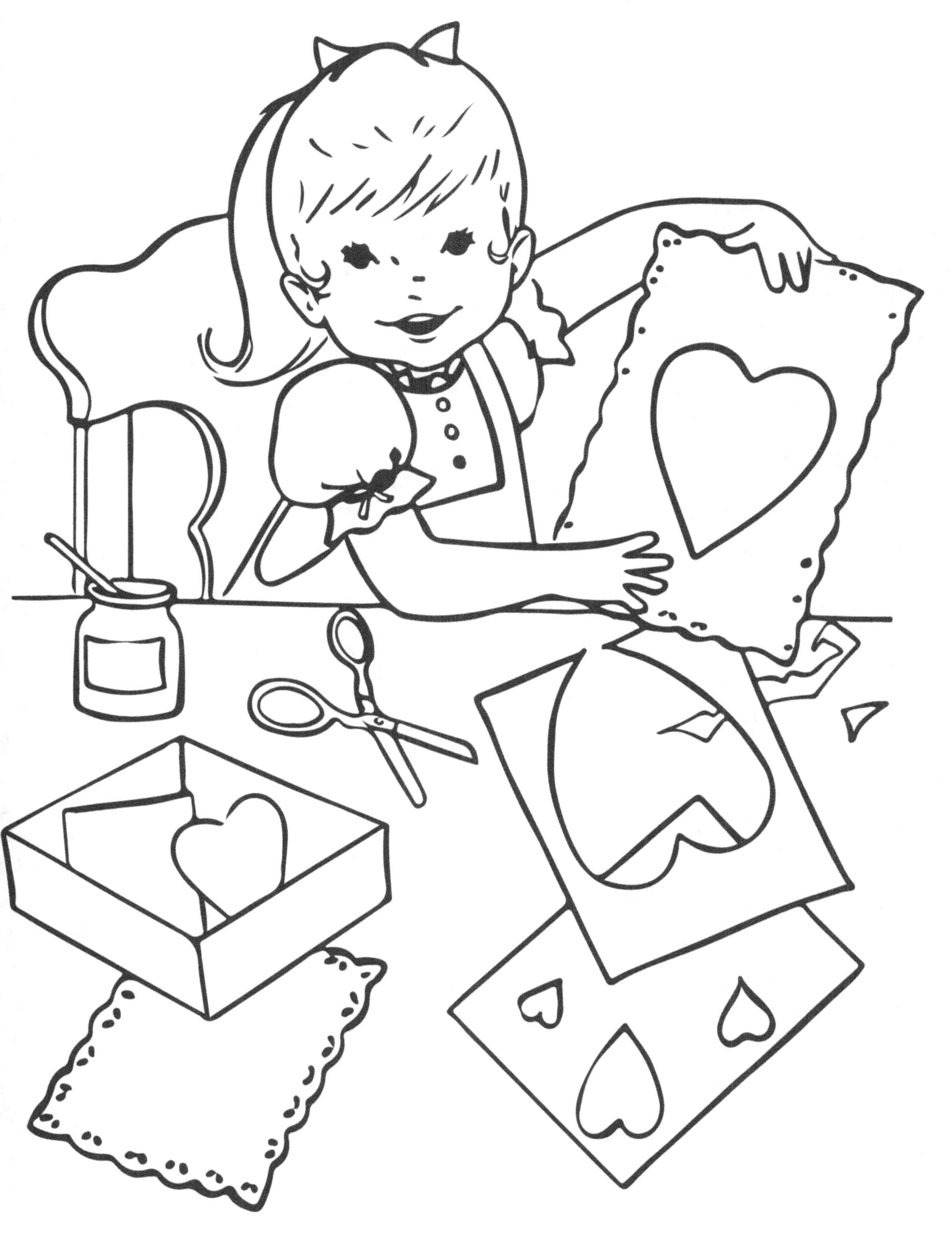

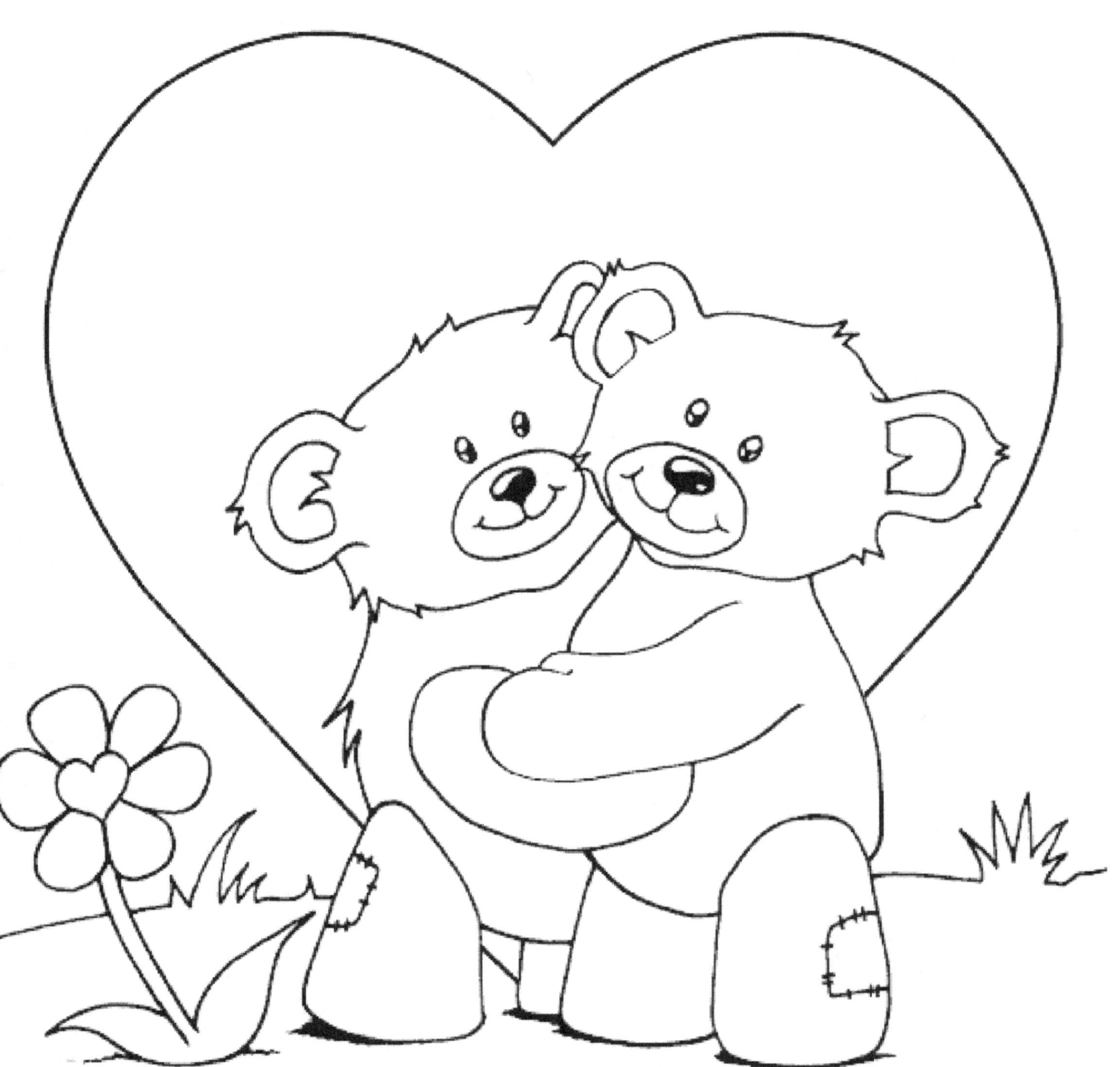

Happy Valentine's Day

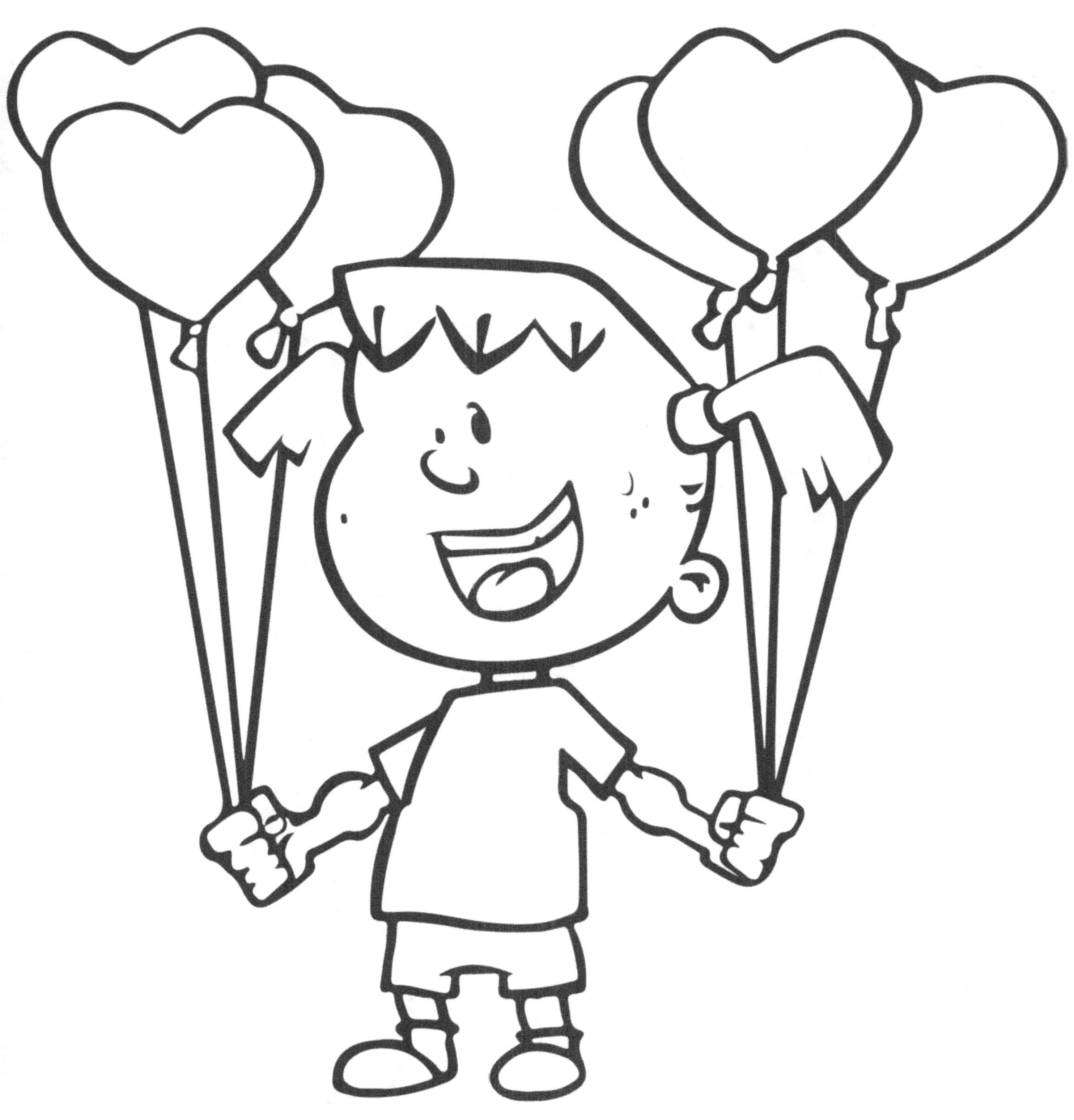

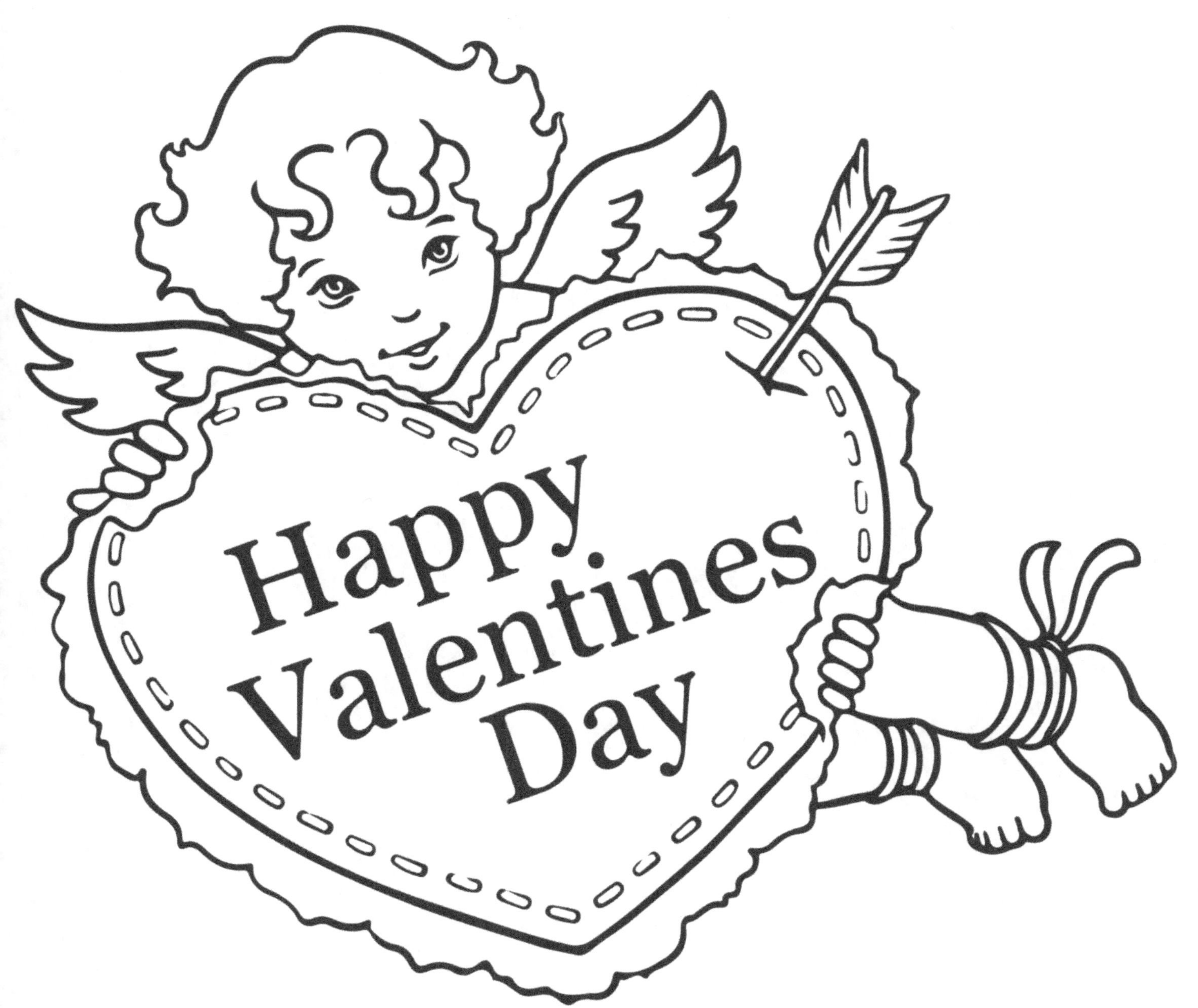
Happy
Valentines
Day

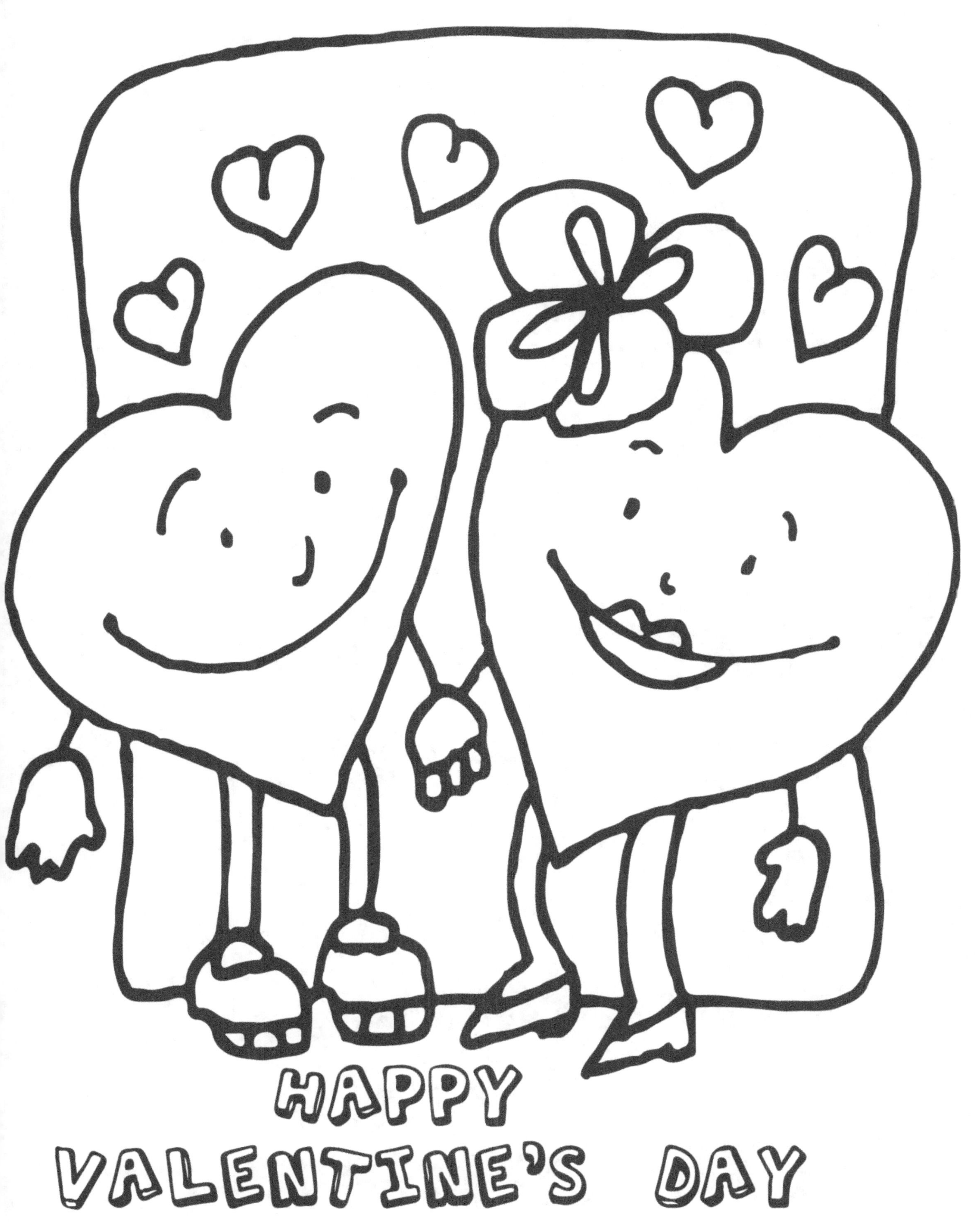

HAPPY
VALENTINE'S DAY

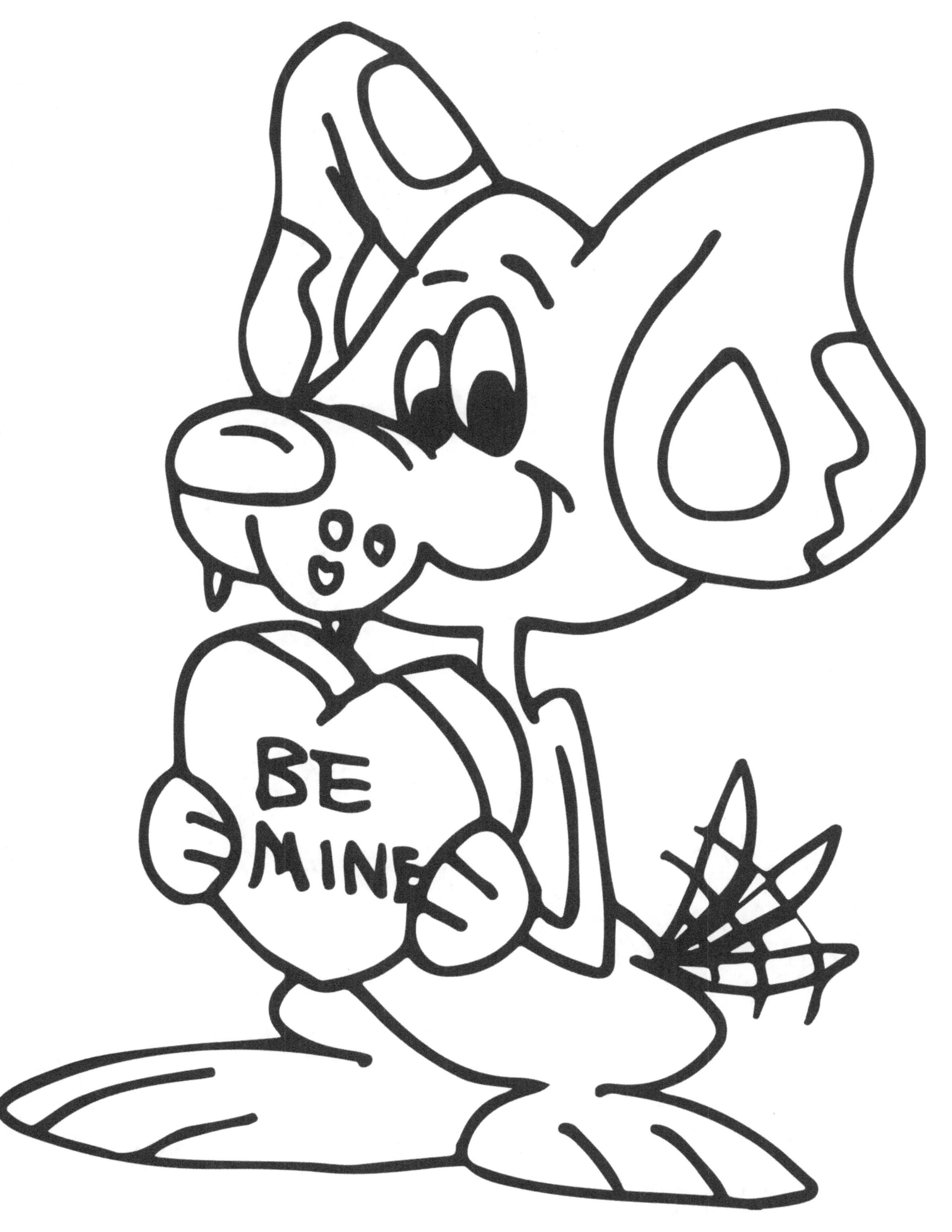

BE
MINE

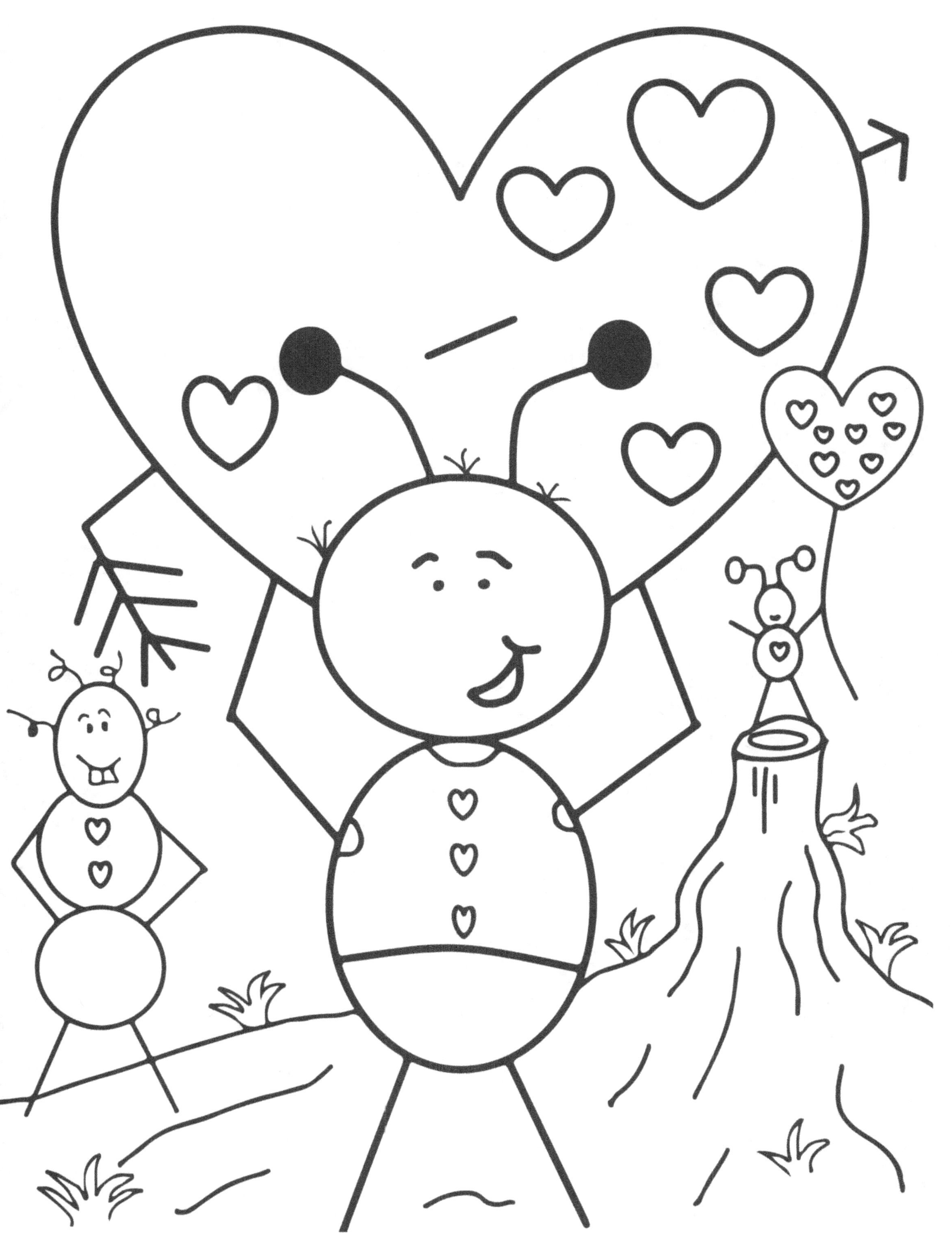

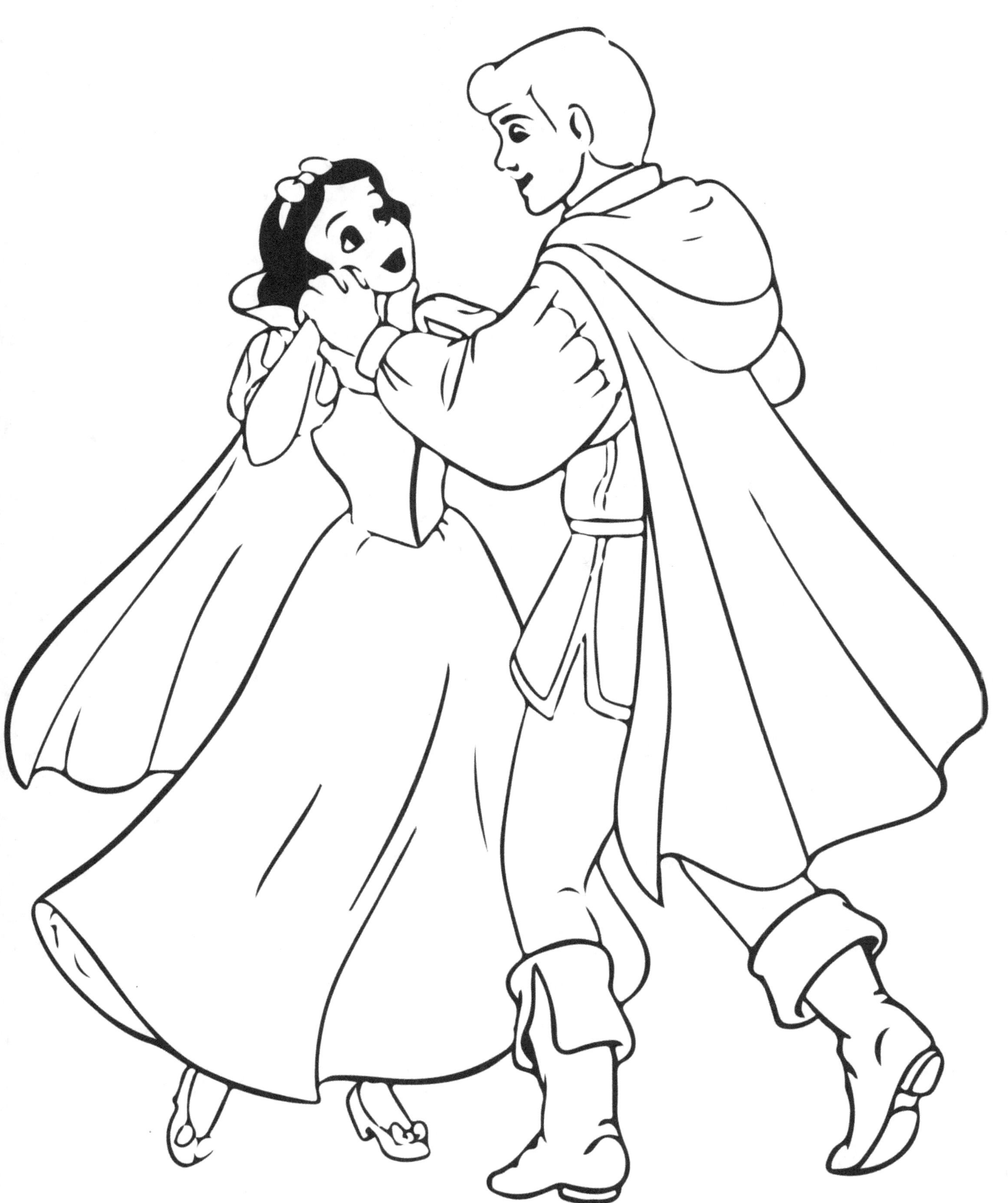

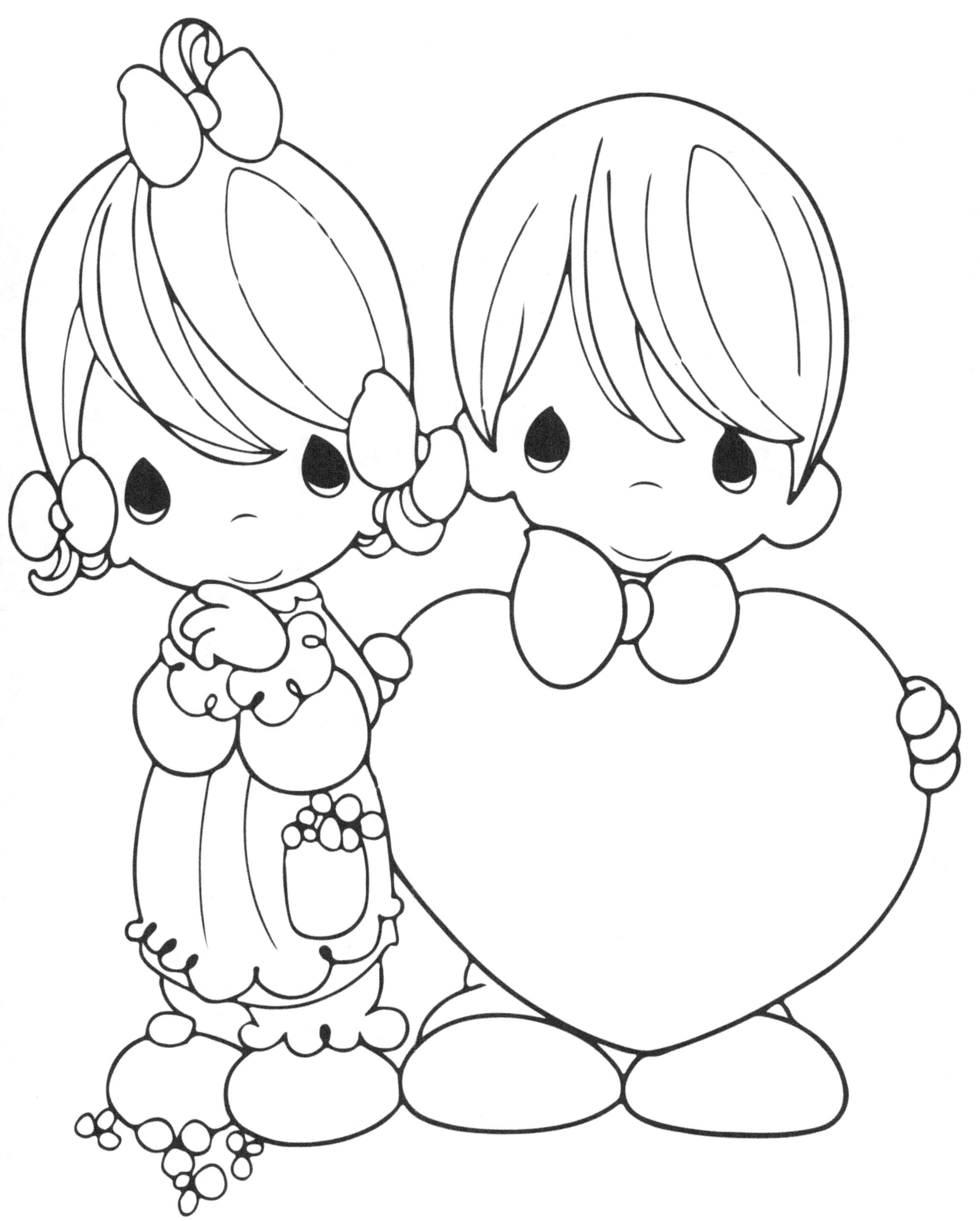

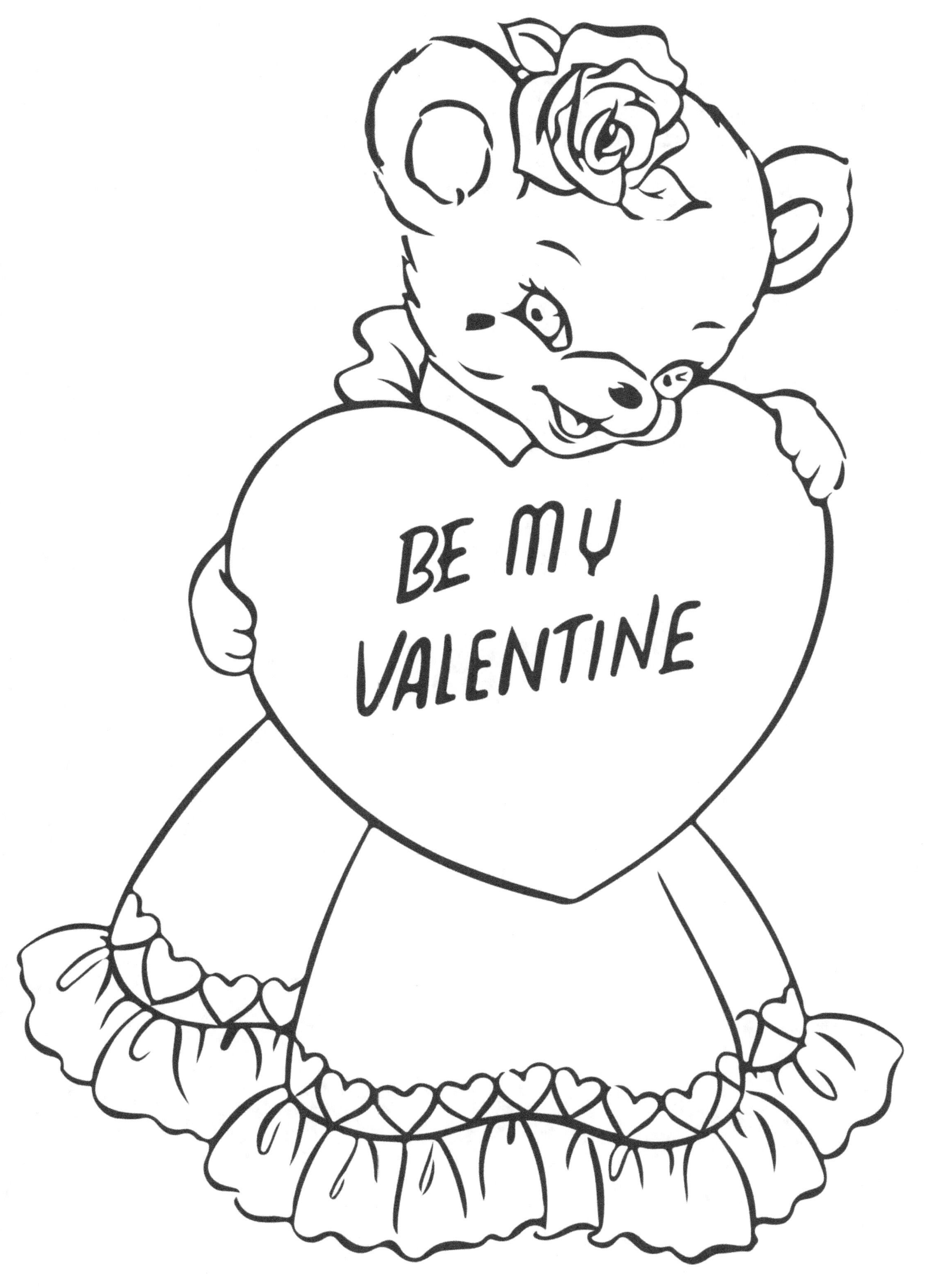

BE MY
VALENTINE

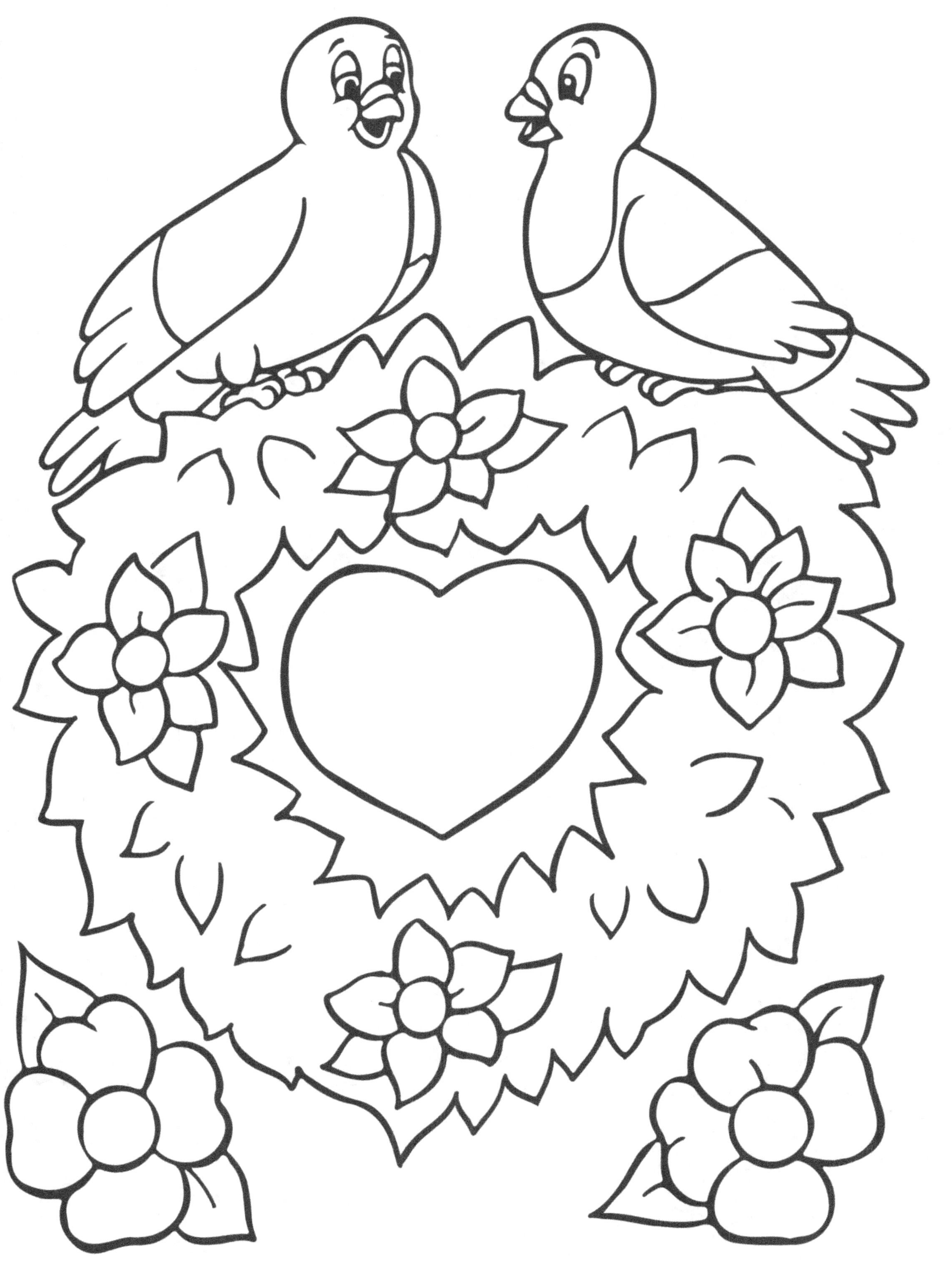

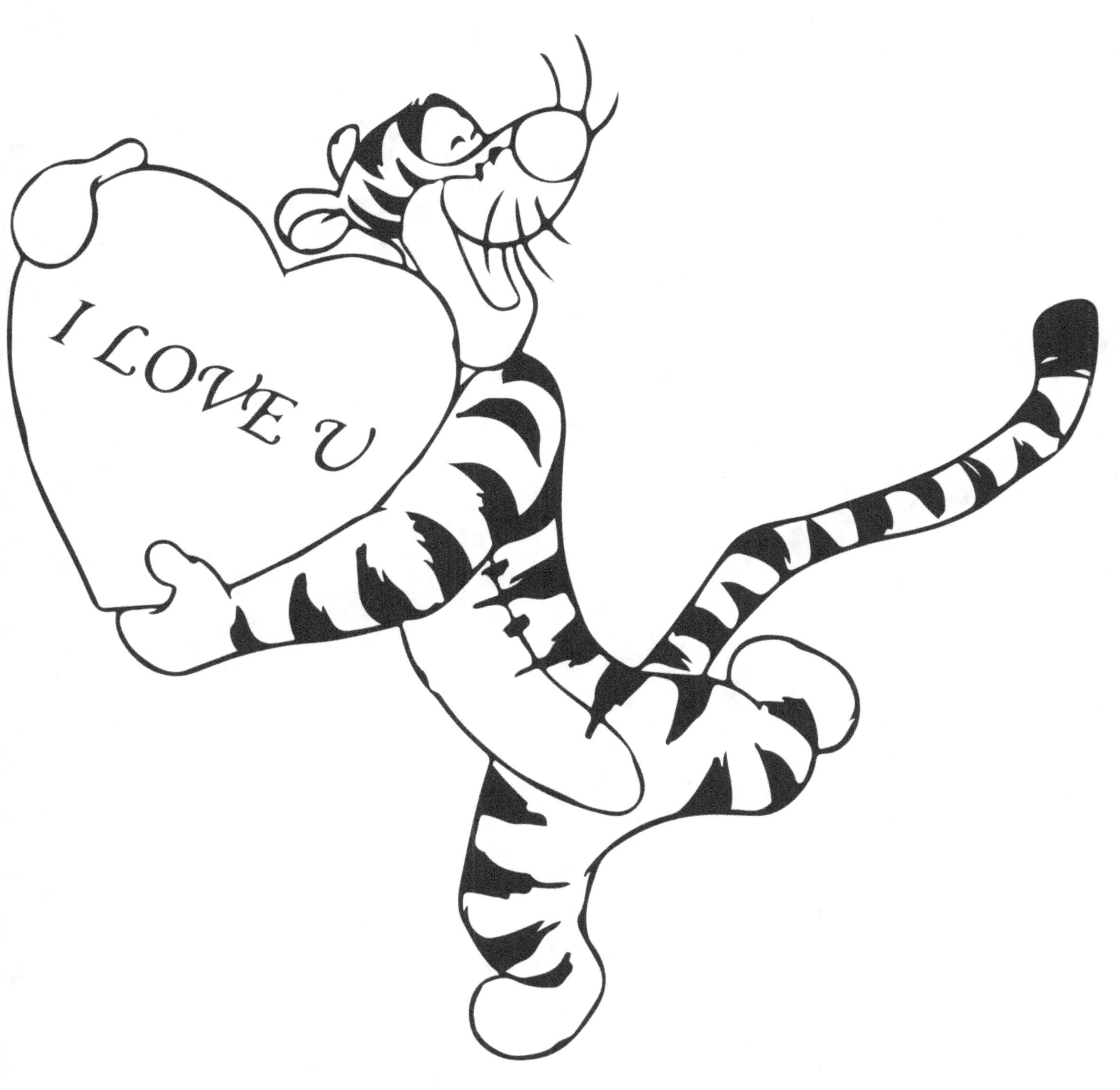

I LOVE U

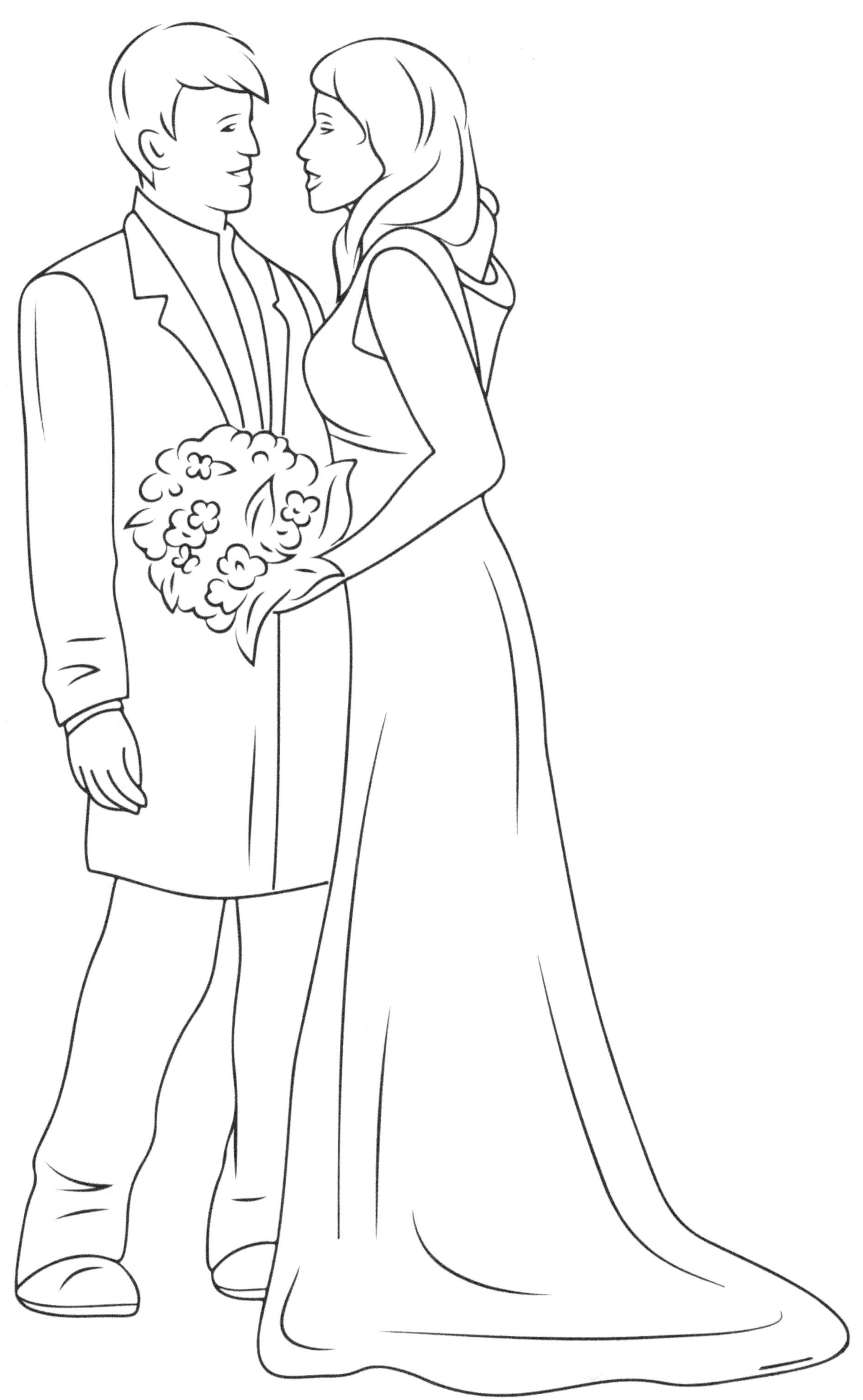

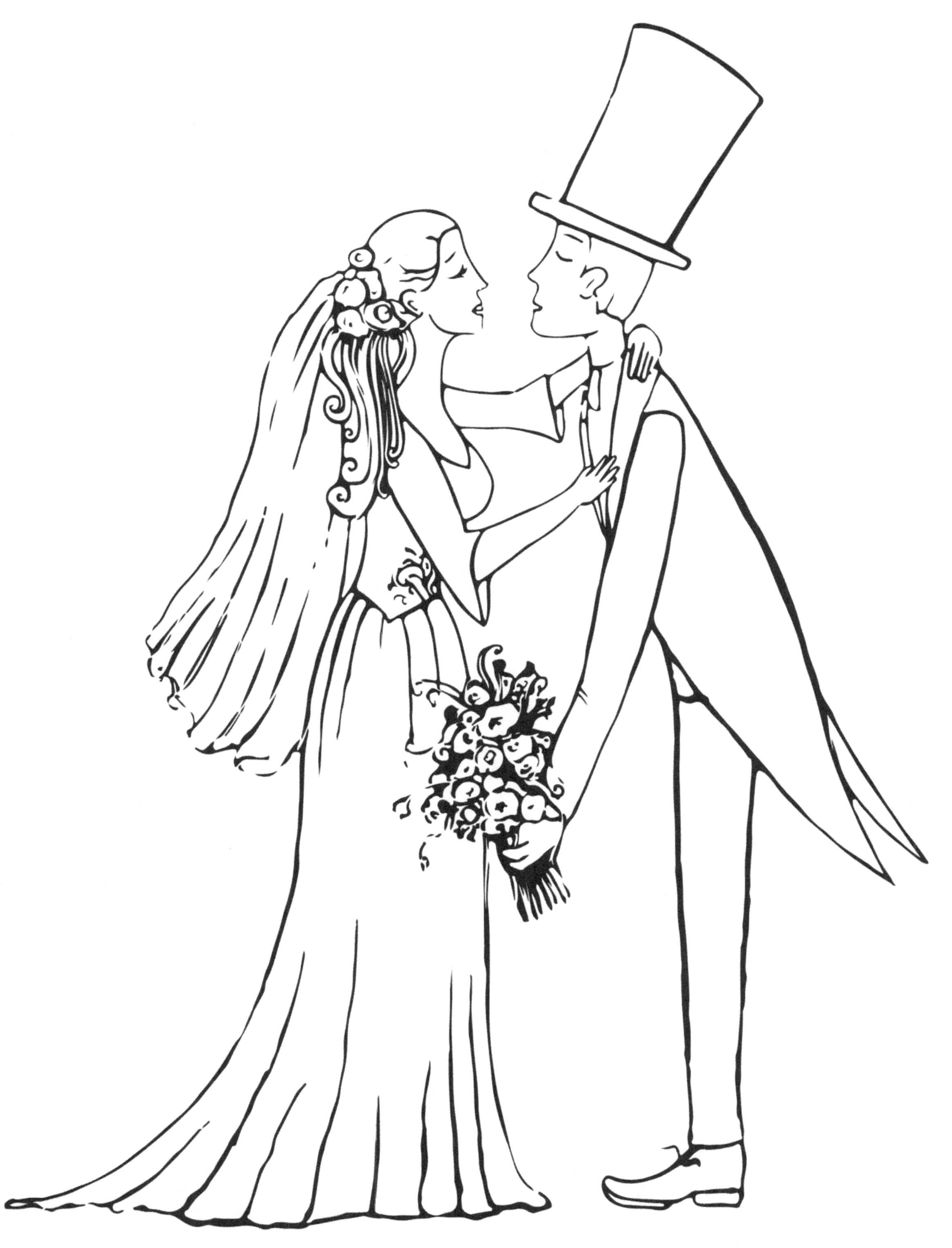

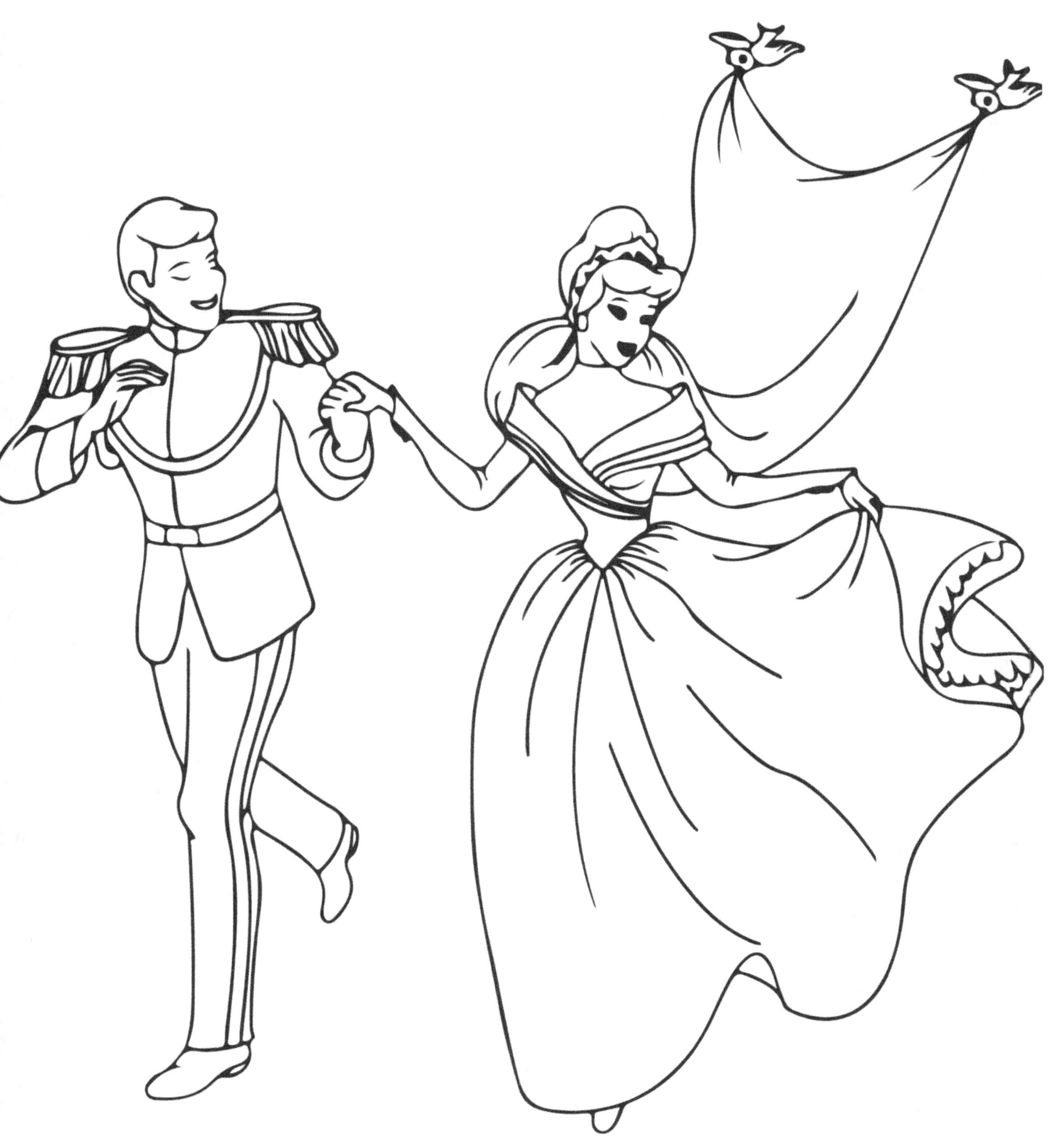

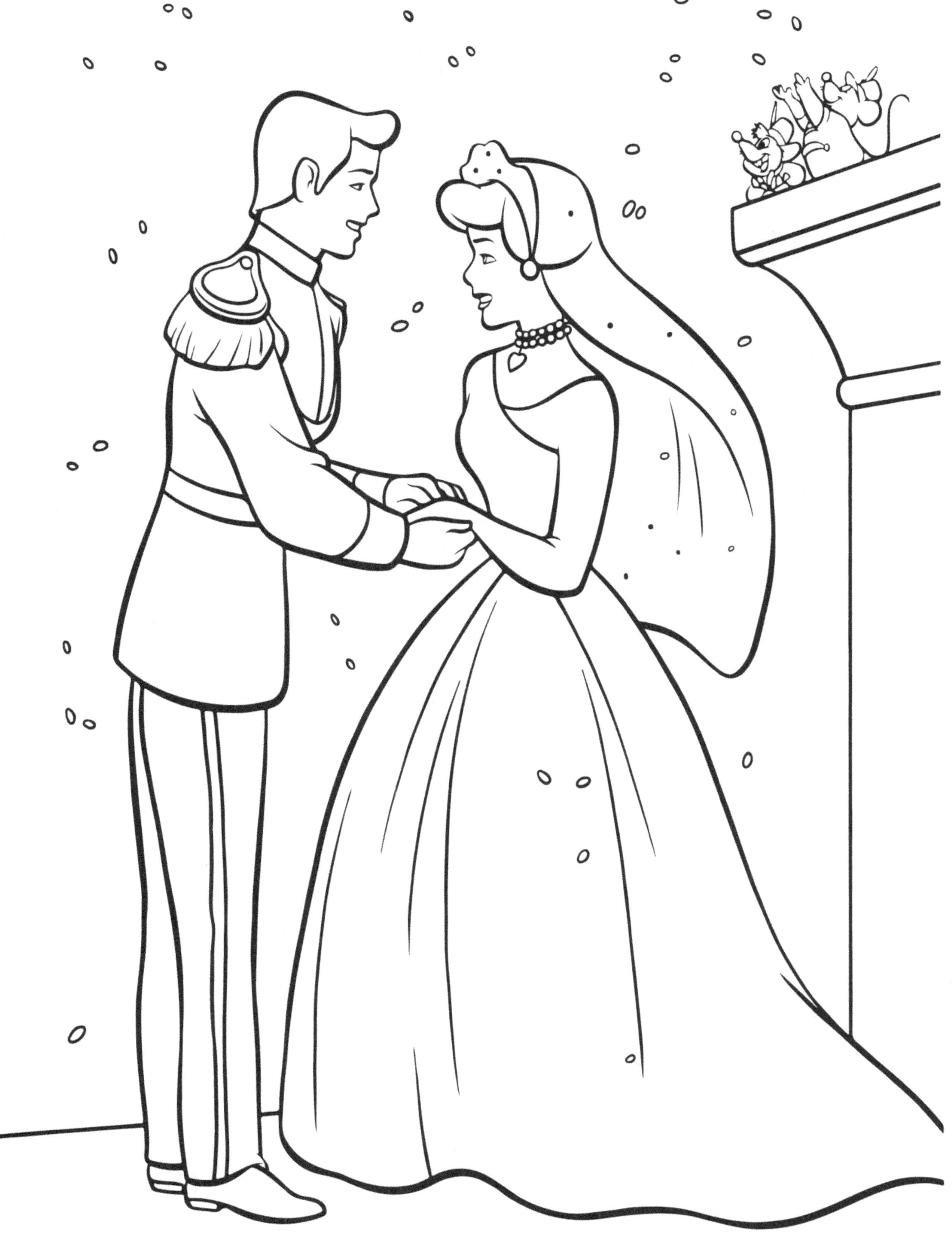

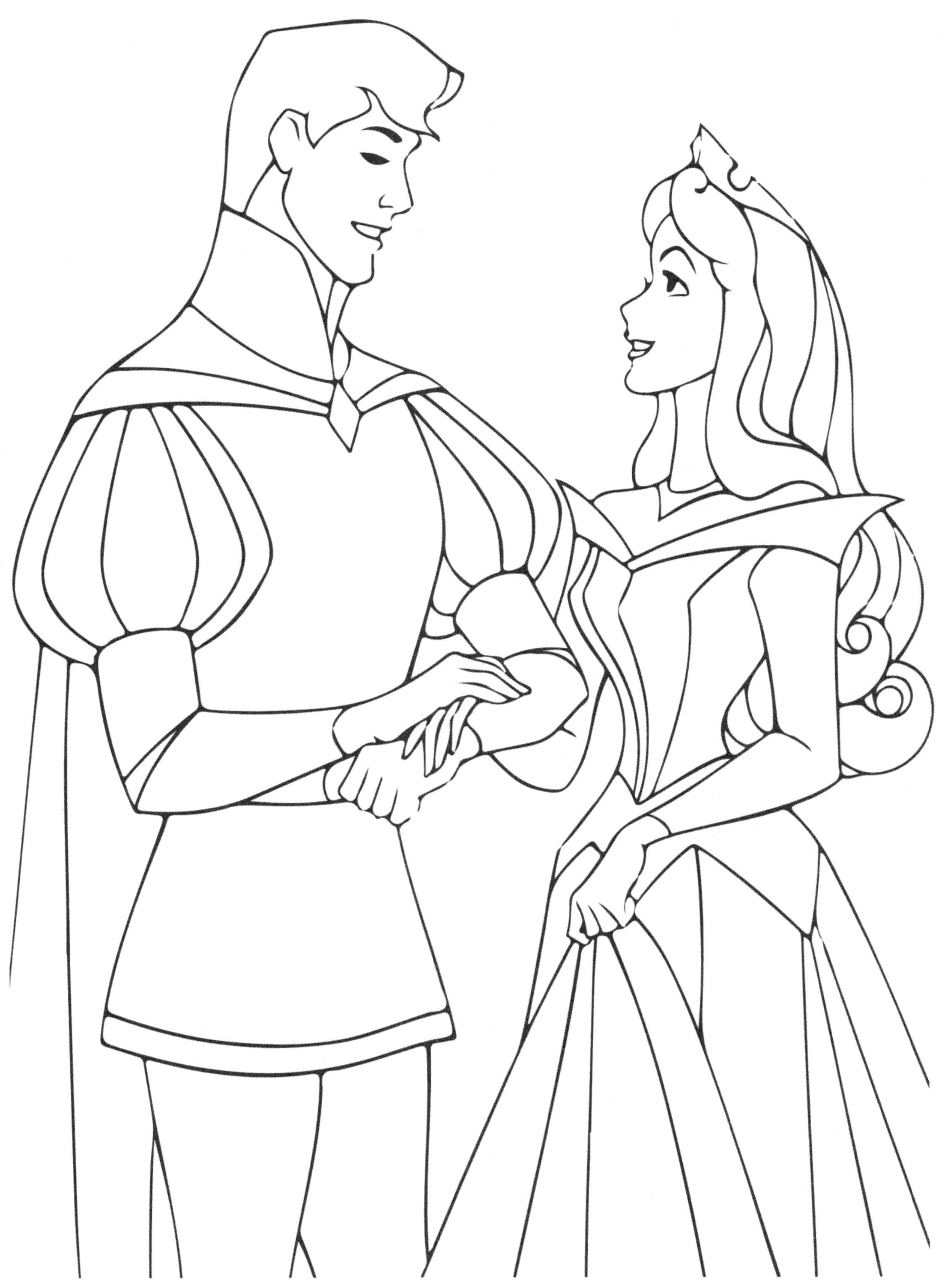

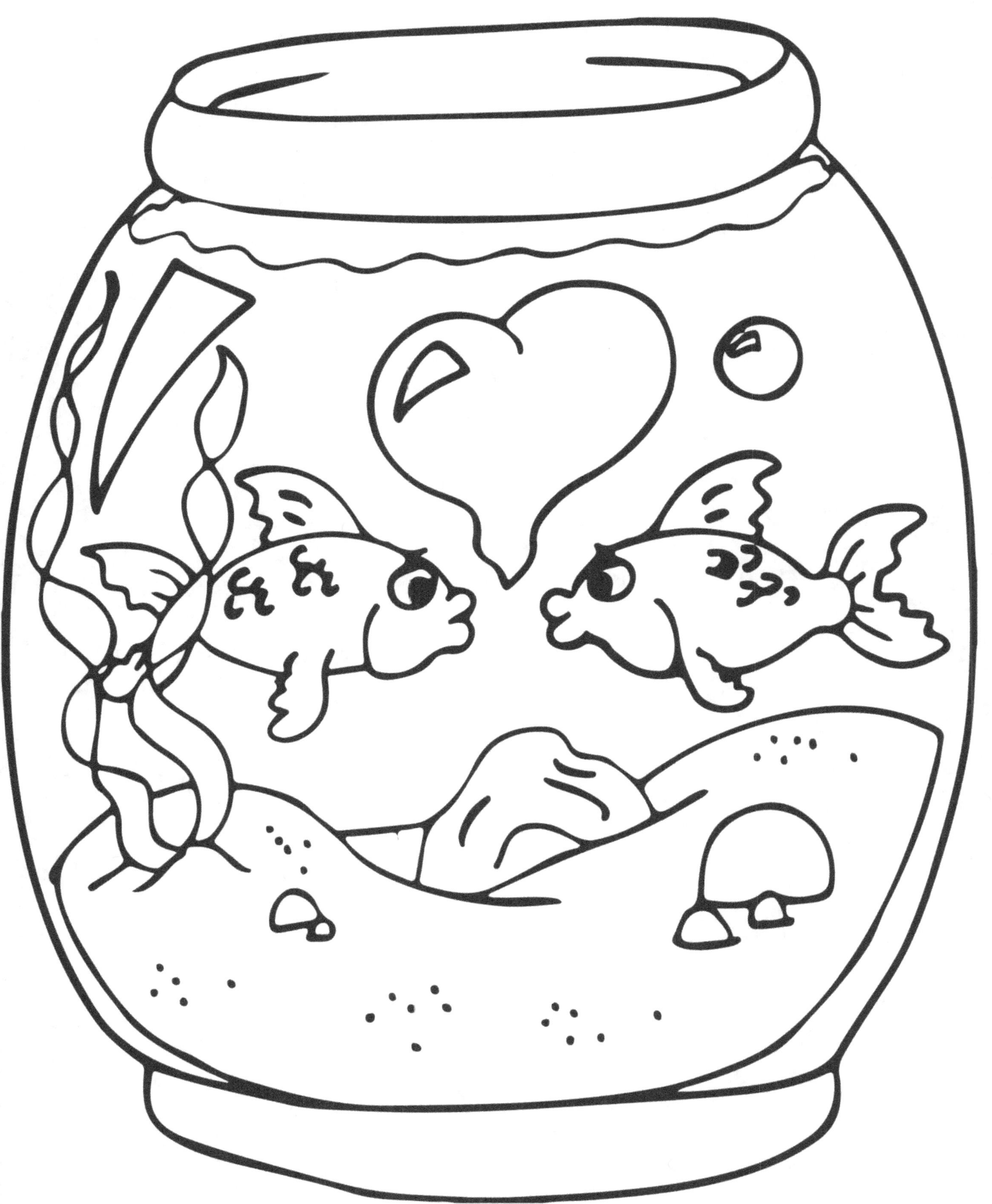

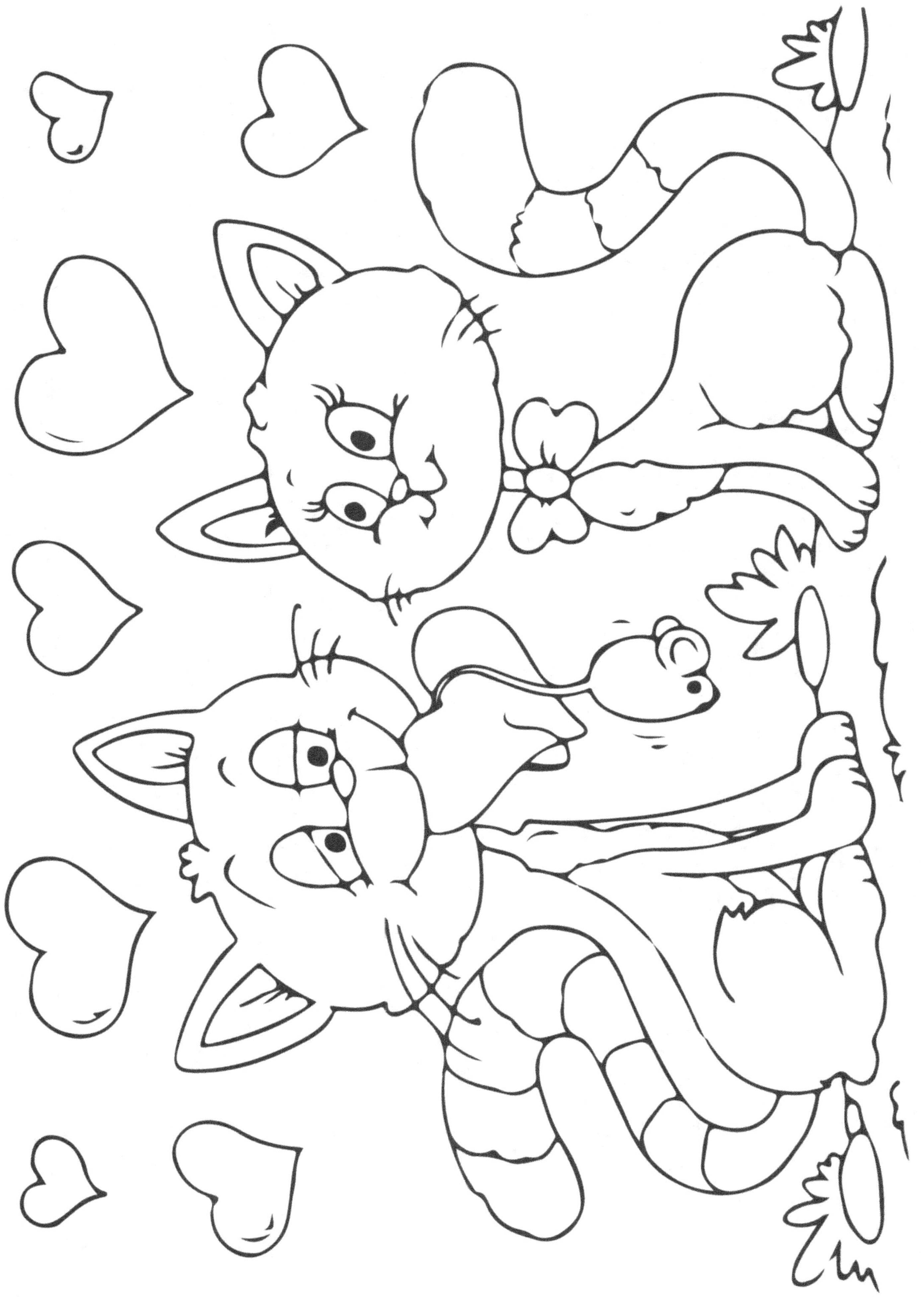

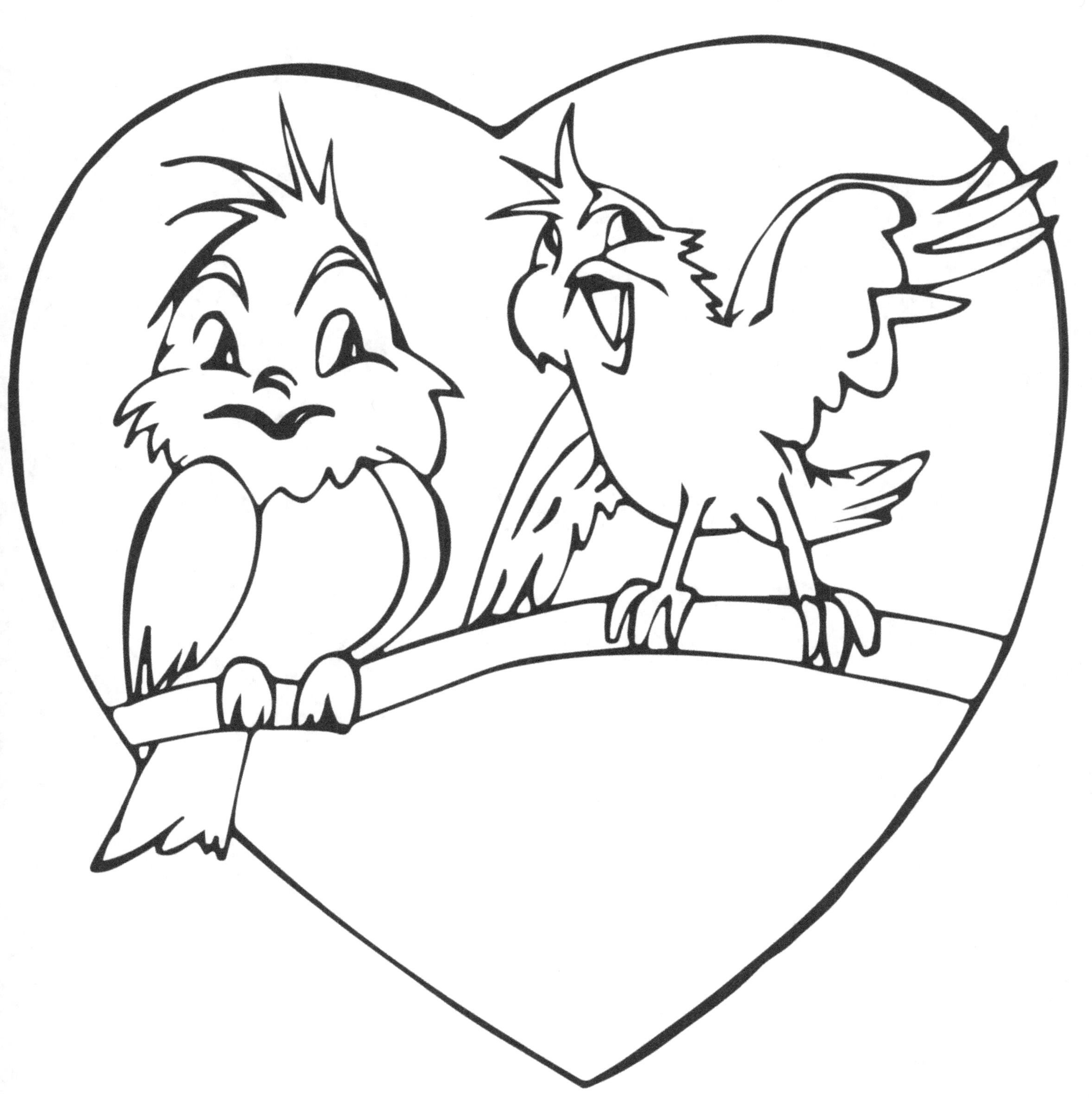

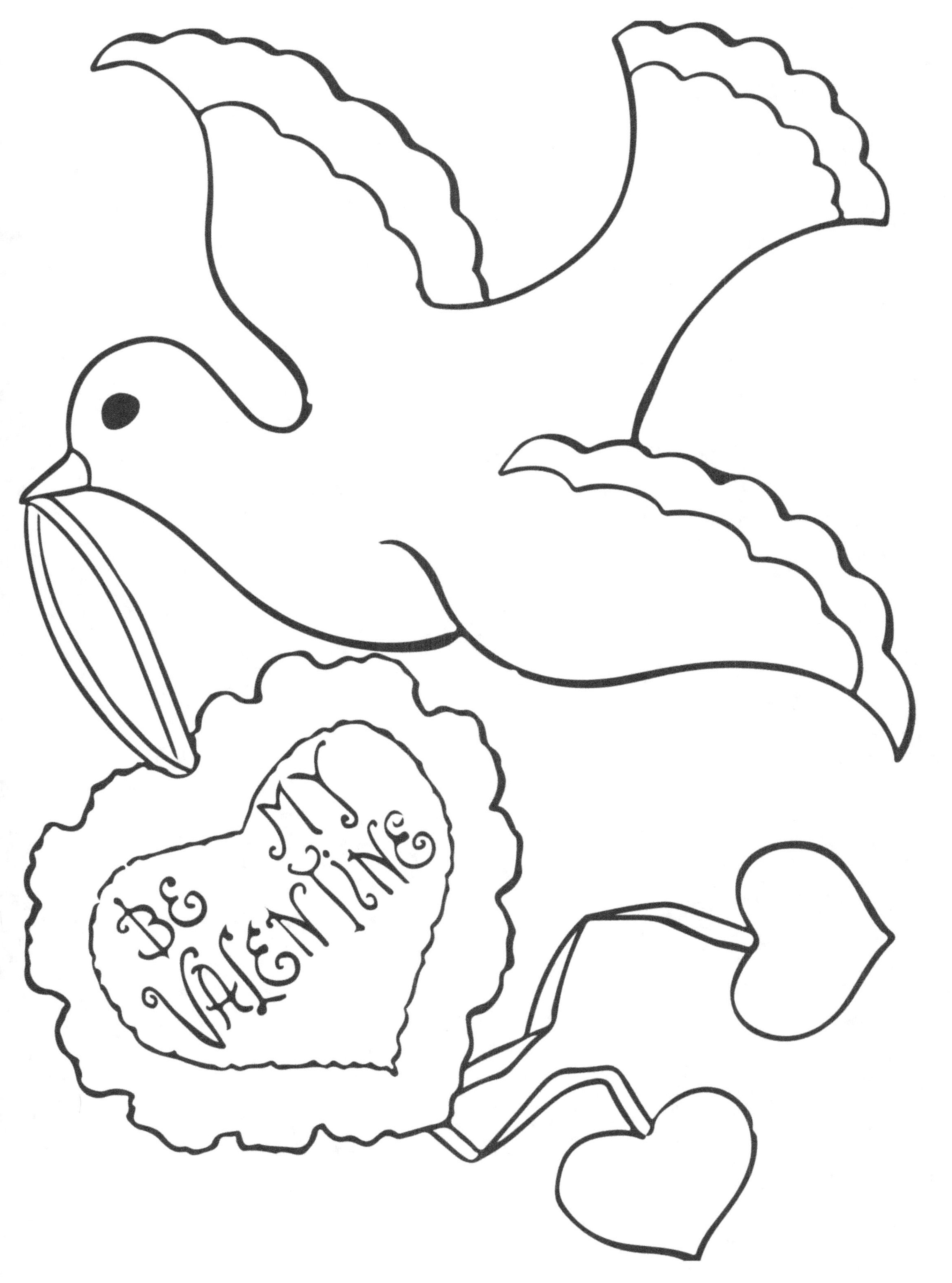

BE MY VALENTINE

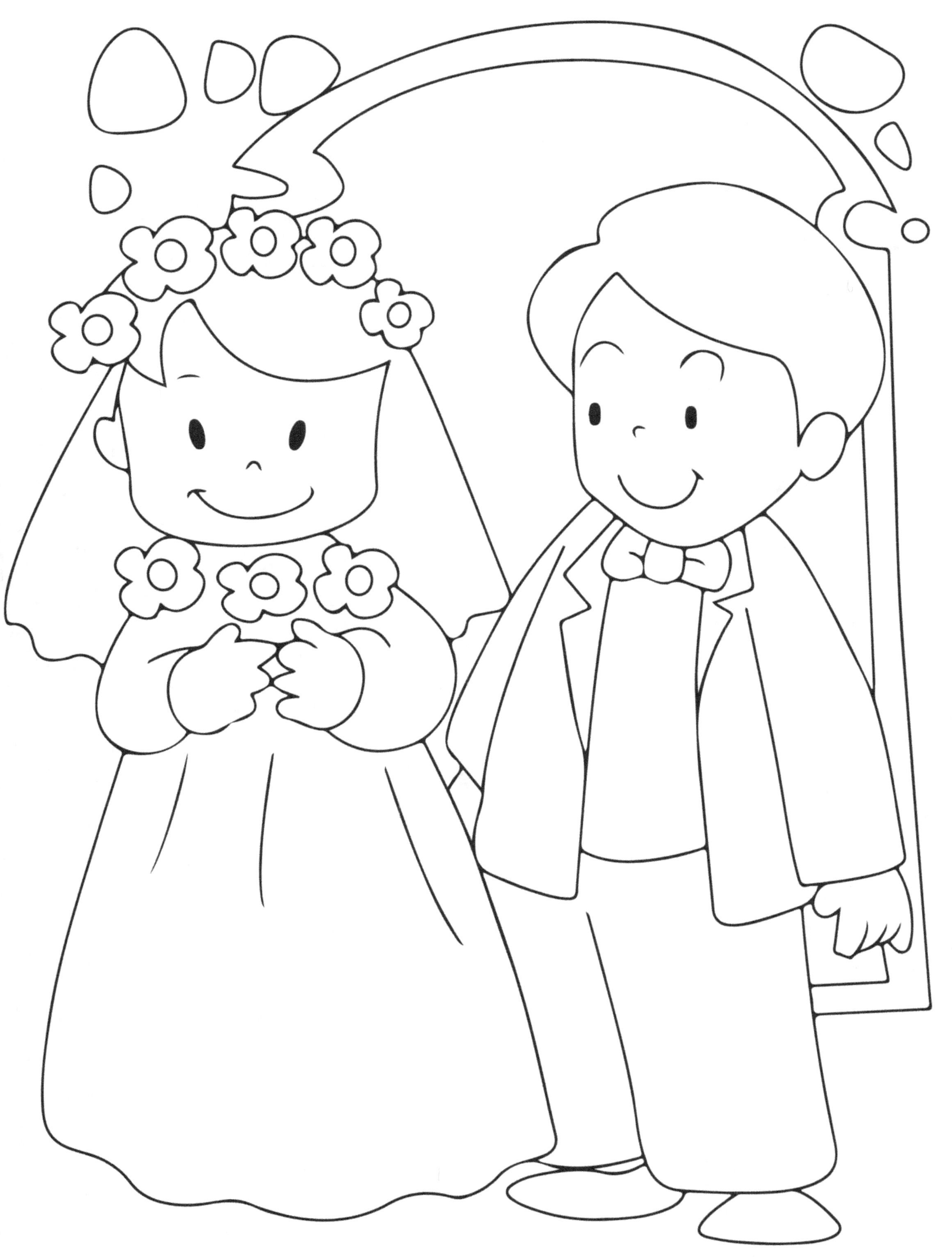

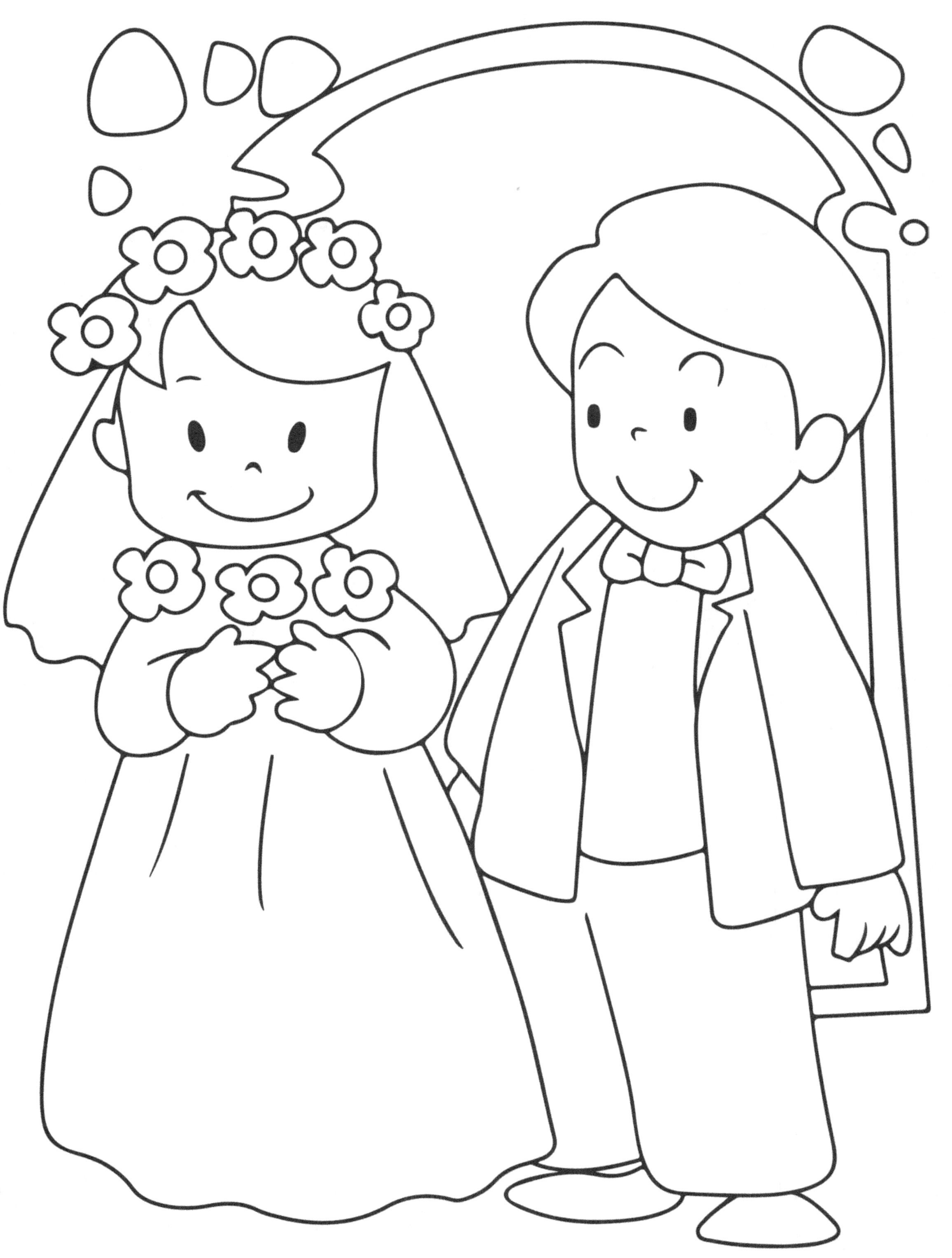

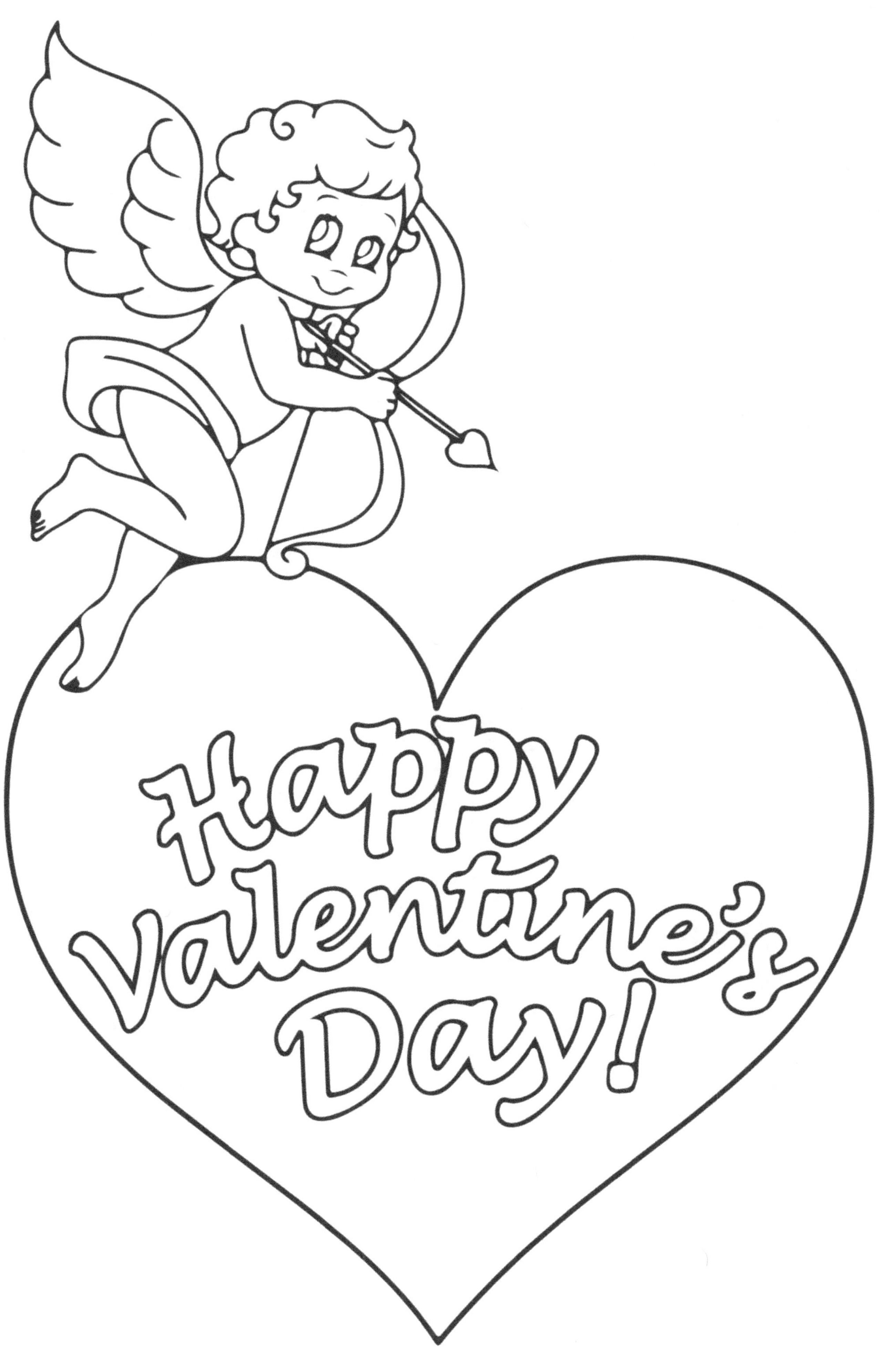

Happy
Valentine's
Day!

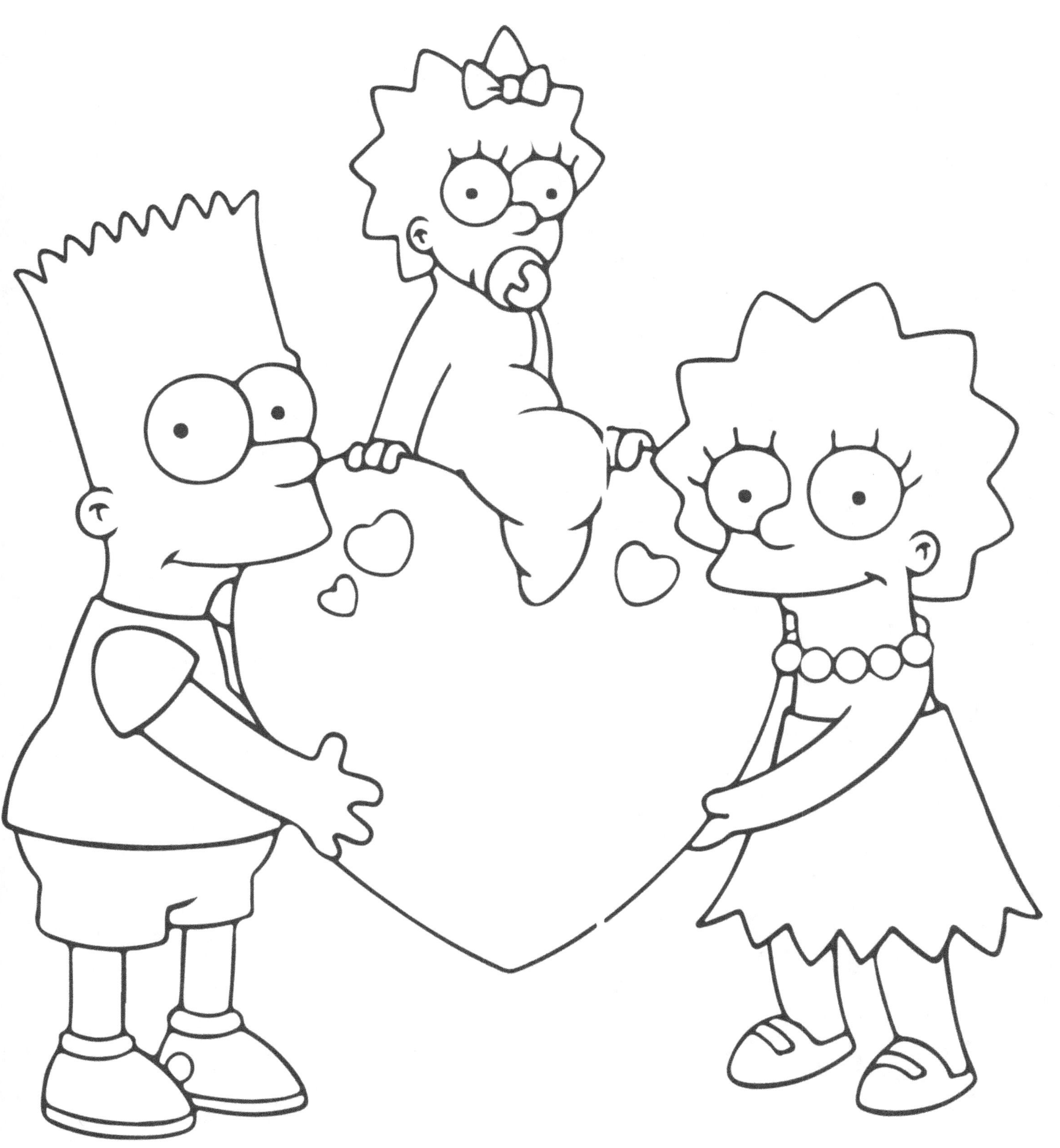

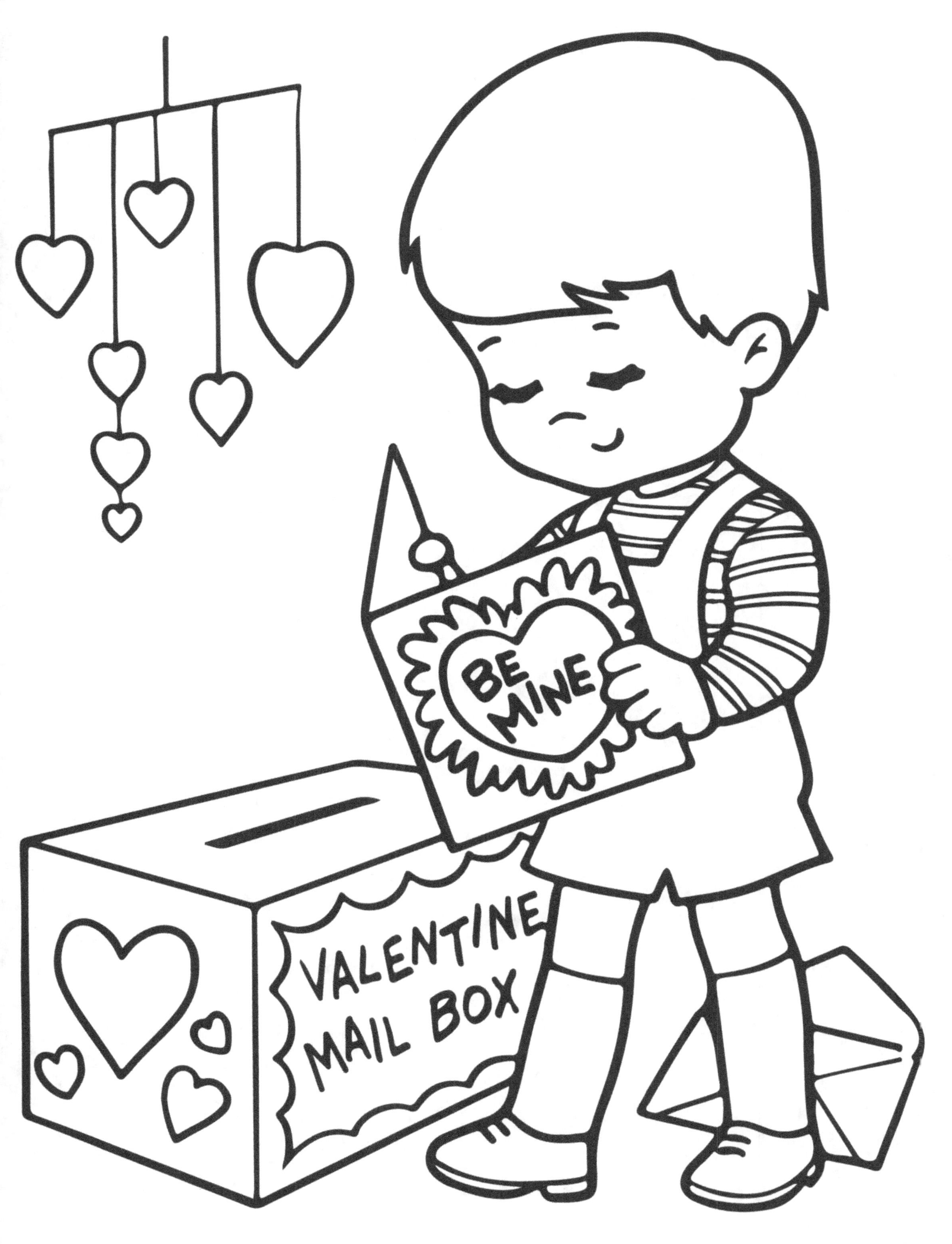

BE MINE
VALENTINE MAIL BOX